WAKE UP Soon! THE TRUMPET WILL Sound!

TAKE THE TIME TO MAKE AN ETERNAL INVESTMENT!

NICOLE LAFERRIÈRE

Print information available on the last page

Rev. date: 03/10/2015

To order additional copies of this book, contact:
Xlibris
1-888-795-4274
www.Xlibris.com
Orders@Xlibris.com

CONTENTS

My Testimony

At 26 years old, I had the privilege and the Grace of God to accept, by faith in my life, the message of the Good News.

The Good News was that I needed to be saved to have eternal life with God who created me. I accepted Jesus Christ into my heart and asked Him to forgiven my sins. Immediately, I received His Spirit and became a new creation in Jesus Christ. It was for me a new beginning of life and I felt His love. He forgave me of all my sins the day I repented. My daily walk made me grow in faith and in the knowledge of His Words.

I had just found out that my son Simon was mentally handicapped but right away, I decided to trust Jesus and I told Him: "With You Jesus, we will go through this together, with Your Love and Your Spirit who strengthens me. Today, I know that my son Simon is, for me, a source of inspiration because I know that I would not be where I am today in my walk with Jesus if it was not for him in my life. For me, Simon is an angel that God sent me to be closer to Him, so that I can give Him all the Glory and the praise.

Thank you Jesus for Simon, for my spouse, my two other children and my grandson! Thank You for making me grow in your love every day!

"…that Christ came into the world to save sinners…" 1 Timothy 1:15

2

Wake Up Soon the Trumpet Will Sound

Wake up soon the trumpet will sound

Wake up soon the trumpet will sound

Tribulation signs you can see all around

The fire of the Lord will soon come down.

Today is the day, Jesus is the way

Repent of your sins, accept Him today

Your name will be written in the book of Life

And you will have eternal life.

Jesus Christ He died now He arise

For you to be saved a perfect sacrifice

If you wait tomorrow it could be too late

Because you don't know if you will be awake

The antichrist will come with the mark of the beast

On your forehead or your hand you will receive

If you accept it you will be deceived

The lack of fire you will receive

I wrote that song that you may know the truth

You have all to gain and nothing to lose

Because the word of God is the only truth

And you are the one who will have to choose

If you want to listen to this song, go on Youtube

(Wake Up Soon by Nicole Laferrière)

The Investment of my Eternal Life

When we live on the earth, we invest in our future. We want to make sure that we have what we need when we are elderly. This is good but that will end when we died.

But how much do we invest in our eternal life which while we're on earth? The only thing that we will bring with us is the richness of our heart.

Every time we take the time to read the Word of God, to pray, and to take the time to be in the presence of the Lord, this is what it will be our investment for eternity.

The love we share, the joy in our heart, and the trust we put in God will have rewards in Heaven.

Every seed that we plant, when we pray, help others, give money to help starving children in other countries, and visit the sick, this "investment" will return to us 100% and more.

Every spiritual investment will have a reward in Heaven. We have to make time to invest for our eternal life.

"…And thus we shall always be with the Lord." 1 Thessalonians 4:17

The Grace of God

The Grace of God is a gift that He gave us when He sent Jesus on earth to come as the Perfect Lamb to be given for our sins.

He was the perfect sacrifice on the Cross to shed His blood so that whoever believes in Him will be saved.

It is a Gift of God. Nobody can save themselves by their good works or by any other form of goodness.

We need the only salvation there is and it is Jesus Christ who provides it.

Jesus is the Way, the Truth and the Life; no one can go to the Father except through Jesus our Saviour.

A **gift** is **free**; you cannot buy a gift. You can only accept it. That is what Grace is; a free gift of God and His Son Jesus is our Saviour and Lord.

When you receive that Grace of God in your life, "Jesus as the only Salvation", you receive eternal life with Jesus. Confess with your mouth the Lord Jesus and believe by faith.

5

What is Faith?

Faith is what you don't see, but whom you believe in. Faith comes from what you hear and what you hear is the Word of God.

When you receive Jesus in your life, you become born again and the Spirit of God reveals to you the Scriptures of God's Word.

All Scripture is inspired by God. Every prophecy in the Old Testament has been accomplished for us to see the coming of Jesus Christ on the Mountain of Olives, **very soon.**

Surround your life by faith in Jesus and you will find peace, joy and an assurance of Eternal Life with Him.

When you ask in prayer for something, believe that you receive it. If it is God's plan, you will receive in His time. But if you ask something and there is doubt in your heart, it is like you didn't ask for anything.

Faith is to believe without doubting; if you want more faith just read the Bible and your faith will grow.

"So then faith comes by hearing, and hearing by the word of God."
Romans 10:17

How to Define Real Love

Love is infinite and endless because love is everything that is good.

Love doesn't envy; it blesses and is always ready to forgive.

Love forgives a multitude of sins and gives life to all who surround you. You are the only one who can work on it because you are the only master of your live every day.

When somebody has hurt you with their words or their thoughts, only you can bless that person to set them free. When you forgive, you have victory because you don't let your heart despair.

Love doesn't bring up the past, mistakes, because love knows how to erase them. It is only in your heart you will have victory because love is the foundation of Faith.

You have received the Love of God when you received your new birth because it is the fruit of the Holy Spirit who produces it.

By reading the Word of Truth, God's Power, you will gain the strength needed to have victory over the enemy.

Friendship

Friendship, an unconditional fraternal Love, is a Love that does not judge or condemn, and is always ready to forgive.

True friendship is enjoying spending time with each other; to enjoy their company and never getting bored.

Friendship is not being jealous but being glad and rejoicing for the kindness being shown toward your friend.

Friendship is taking the time to spend together, crying together and comforting each other.

Friendship is precious and nothing can separate or replace real friends.

Happiness

Real happiness is to know You, Jesus Christ, the True God—my Creator—and to accept free salvation through Jesus Christ our Saviour.

All of the things of the earth are only lent to us so that we can live a blessed life on earth. But it is not the riches of the world that will fill our lives. The emptiness that we have in our heart, only Jesus Christ can fill.

We have to surrender our life, body, mind, and soul to Jesus.

Early in the morning we can feel His love when we take the time to talk to Him. He is our Source of inspiration that brings joy, peace, and love in our hearts. Only He can give us real happiness.

Who is Jesus?

Jesus is God, who, having left His Throne in Heaven, came to earth as a human being. He is the Word of God.

His mission, He says, was to come as the Perfect Lamb to be immolated on the Cross for our sins.

Jesus who had no any sins came to save us. He is the only Saviour. "He is the Way, the Truth and the Life. No one can come to the Father except through Jesus." John 14:6

Before Jesus came as a human being, He was with the Father. He created everything with God, and before Abraham was, He was. When He gave His life on the Cross, it was only His body as a human being who died. His Spirit never died.

One day, we will be with Him forever, if we accept Him in our hearts as our personal Saviour and Lord of our lives and repent of our sins.

Jesus taught us about God the Father. When He was on earth, He said if you know Me, you also know My Father because We are One.

Jesus wants a personal relationship from us, not a religion. It was God the Father's plan to send us Jesus as the perfect sacrifice to be saved.

Jesus is always there every day and every moment of the day to help us when we call Him.

Jesus' names are:

Alpha & Omega	The Beginning and The End
The Prince of Peace	The King of kings
The Lord of lords	Messiah
The Saviour	Jehovah
Emmanuel (God with us)	Jesus is God

Thank you, Jesus, for coming to save us. Your precious blood has been shed on the Cross for the sins of the whole world. Everyone who calls upon Your name shall be saved.

"For there is one God and one Mediator between God and men, the Man Christ Jesus..."
1 Timothy 2:5

Who is God?

God is everywhere and sees everything in us. He is the Creator of the whole universe and everything under and on the earth. He is all-powerful and He has always existed.

He knows our thinking and every hair of our head is counted. There is nothing He doesn't know.

God is a Spirit and omnipresent; nothing can be hidden from Him.

His love for us is eternal because in His eyes, we are a prize. He wants all the adoration from our lives and our actions.

If we know the Only True God, we will be satisfied because he is majestic. He is always there waiting for us to talk to Him and to have trust in Him. Amen.

He wants a personal relationship with each one of us.

"The whole creation reflects the wisdom of the Glory of God."

"This is the message which we have heard from Him and declare to you, that God is light and in Him is no darkness at all." 1 John 1:5

Who is the Holy Spirit?

The Holy Spirit is the Spirit of God sent for us who are saved. He helps us to know God and He teaches us the truth.

When Jesus returned to the Father, He told us: "I will send you the Helper, the Holy Spirit, who will teach you all that I have taught you while I was on the earth."

Today, it is the Holy Spirit who works in our hearts and transforms our lives. Without the Holy Spirit, we can do nothing because He is our strength.

He testifies to our hearts and makes us walk in the truth of our Saviour Jesus Christ.

We need the Holy Spirit to keep us on the right way. He guides us when we trust in Him and put our lives in His hands.

He teaches us from wrong and transforms our hearts and lives. See 2 Timothy 3:16.

""It is the Spirit who gives life; the flesh profits nothing. The words that I speak to you are spirit, and they are life." John 6:63

What is the Resurrection?

In the Bible, Jesus talks about the resurrection telling us it is a new life after death.

There is no place in the Scriptures where reincarnation is mentioned. Jesus resurrected from the dead and we also will be resurrected.

In the day of the Judgment, the just will be resurrected to eternal life with Jesus, and for those who did not accept Jesus as their personal Saviour and Lord and did not repent of their sins, they will have eternal life with Satan, the devil and his angels of darkness.

Jesus is good and merciful, but He is also just and true.

It is now, while we are alive, that we have the chance to accept Jesus in our lives. It is not when we will be dead. "Make your choice."

The Word of God said: "If you confess the Lord Jesus Christ with your mouth and if you believe that He was resurrected from the dead, you will be saved."

It is not by your good works, it is only by grace through Jesus Christ our Saviour and by faith.

The moment that you accept Jesus in your life, He gives you assurance of eternal life in your heart. The Holy Spirit lives in you for eternity. Your name is written in the Lamb's Book of Life. He prepares you a place for you to be with Jesus for eternity.

We will live in the New Jerusalem where all is beauty and riches. There will be no more tears and everything is pure. Satan will not be there to deceive people. Only the holy ones will be there.

God sees us pure, holy and without blemish through His Son Jesus Christ.

There is no more condemnation for the one who is born of the Spirit of God.

Jesus is the Only One who can forgive our sins because He is "…the way, the truth and the life." John 14:6

"Jesus said to her, "I am the resurrection and the life. He who believes in Me, though he may die, he shall live." John 11:25

What is Forgiveness?

Forgiveness is the gift to be set free and set other people free. Without forgiveness, you are imprisoned. You have a hard time to look at the person that upsets you and you feel hardness in your heart.

When we are not able to forgive it is because we are not able to forgive ourselves.

The Bible tells us to forgive the one who offends us, not

7 times but 7 x 70 times. It is with the help of Almighty God that we can do this.

This is the only way that we can achieve forgiveness when we put our trust in Jesus, and in His hands we surrender everything in our lives to Him.

There will be peace and joy that will come in your hearts. Nobody else can set you free. Jesus is the answer to all your problems, and He will give you peace in your heart when you forgive.

"And be kind one to another, tenderhearted, forgiving one another, even as God in Christ forgave you." Ephesians 4:32

The Invisible God

The invisible God is made visible through Jesus Christ because God is fully present in Jesus Christ, as well as with the Holy Spirit who was in the Beginning and is for all Eternity.

It is through a personal relationship with the living God that we acknowledge that we are sinners and that we need a Saviour.

When Jesus died on the cross it was a perfect sacrifice that nobody else could accomplish. Jesus gave Himself for the whole world and for our redemption. Now we have a choice to make: To accept Jesus or to refuse Jesus.

It is a free gift from God. We all have to gain by accepting Him. This gift will give you Eternal Life with Jesus. But to refuse Him will bring eternal condemnation with all the evils.

The only sins that cannot be forgiven are to refuse Jesus as your personal Saviour and to refuse the Holy Spirit into your life.

The bread that we eat every day is for our body and it will die. But the Word of God is our spiritual bread that will keep our spirit alive for eternity.

Why Sing?

Singing is a source of inspiration that sets you free and gives you strength. This is a very good medicine to take for your life.

When you are tired, oppressed, and sad in your heart, start singing praises to God and you will find happiness.

Early in the morning, the birds sing to the Glory of God. So why don't you sing to our Lord Jesus to praise and worship Him.

Jesus fills us with His Love and takes away the fear in our hearts. "The joy of the Lord is my strength."

He is my Shepherd and I will not fear. I hear His voice that fills my spirit with His Love because He is eternal Love.

What is the Real Truth?

The truth is found in the word of God because He gives it to us so that we will know the truth.

Every word that we find in the Bible is from the inspiration of the Holy Spirit of God. All the circumstances of life are found in His Word for us to know what we should do with our lives.

We have to believe His Word by faith for it to work in our lives.

It is our own choice to read it for ourselves as it is our heritage that God gives us.

The truth is not always easy to say; sometimes it hurts to hear it, but it is the truth that will set you free.

"For the word of God is living and powerful, and sharper than any two-edged sword, piercing even to the division of soul and spirit, and of joints and morrow, and is a discerner of the thoughts and intents of the heart."

Hebrews 4:12

Divorce

When we got married, love was between us. The years went by and the struggles of life came and destroyed us; the love that we had for each other had brought us together. But after the years of pain and suffering, it became like a fire between us.

The day that we "yes" to each other before God, we thought it would be for life.

But through the years, the enemy came to destroy our union. To restore our marriage, there is only one who can help us and it is Jesus Christ.

Through all the circumstances and sufferings that we face every day, we can receive help if we surrender our lives in the hands of the Lord Jesus Christ.

When we put all our trust in the Word of God by faith, He will give us everlasting Joy in our lives.

When You Feel Oppressed

In your everyday life, you give your love to everyone who surrounds you, but you feel the oppression and sense false accusations within you.

These false accusations do not belong to you but they cause you to feel oppressed. Don't keep those negative words that want to crush you and keep you down. Reject them far from you and don't meditate on those negative words; you have to let them go.

You have the choice to keep them so that they stop you from functioning, but you also have the power to reject them and to be set free.

The negative words keep your mind in darkness and your heart gets harder. They prevent you from seeing the beauty in your heart that God has given you. Jesus' words of truth (The Bible) renew your mind and sets you free from darkness, making you more than a conqueror with the Lord Jesus Christ.

If you confess with your mouth the Lord Jesus Christ and believe in your heart that He is the Saviour, you will have the victory on all the oppression in your life.

Jesus is present in your life every day to confront the enemy.

What is the purpose reincarnation?

Reincarnation has been invented by humans and there is nowhere in the Bible that this subject is mentioned.

It is a belief accepted by people who are afraid to die. Their conscience lies to them and they believe the lie that the enemy wants them to believe.

Since Jesus has resurrected, we also will resurrect. There are only two places that we can go; Heaven or Hell. The people who believe in reincarnation don't believe in Hell. Their belief makes them think that they will have second chance to come back on earth so that they can try to have a better life.

The Bible says: "And as it is appointed for men to die once, but after this the judgment". Hebrews 9:27

For everybody, while living their lives on this earth, have the chance to accept the free salvation and truth of Jesus Christ, and to repent of their sins. This decision has given them the assurance of Eternal Life.

We are all sinners and we need a Saviour. God provided a Saviour, His Son Jesus. God has made us different from all animals and plants. He made us in His own Image and gave us the breath of life.

Our spirit will live for all eternity. We are all unique as His creation and we will receive a new body, a "Holy Body", at the resurrection with the same soul and spirit.

We are the only one who can make the decision for our own life. Jesus gave us the freedom to choose to believe in Him. For the one who believes in Jesus, this makes him or her a child of God.

Satan is the father of lies. He is a liar since the beginning and tries to get as many people to believe in those lies, so that they will follow Him into the pit of fire. He is a deceiver and wants to destroy our lives in any way he can.

Witchcraft, reading palms, fortune telling, and all those things are abomination in the eyes of God. This brings on you not a blessing but it curses your life.

Everyone who refuses the Salvation truth that Jesus Christ offers will be deceived. They will be condemned for eternity because they prefer to believe the enemy's lies instead of the truth of the Gospel.

Everybody will have to face the Throne of God for our beliefs, but we are without excuses because He has left us our heritage "The New Testament" to know the real truth. We are without excuses.

He gives us free will; everything started by faith. We have to make the right choice because there is a consequence.

To believe in reincarnation is not to believe in the Bible. Every word of God has been inspired by the Holy Spirit and it works in the life of the one who believes in it.

Jesus is Love, He forgives us if we repent and He changes us if we surrender our lives in His hands. We have to renounce following Satan and put our trust in the Only True God the Father, Our Saviour Jesus Christ and the Holy Spirit.

Living one day at a time is enough. Don't try to know the future and don't live in the past. We all have to answer for our beliefs and our actions.

When Your Body Dies

When our body dies, our spirit returns to God. Our spirit is eternal and will live forever.

To be separated from the body is to be in the presence of the Lord if you know Jesus as your personal Saviour and Lord of your life.

It is destined for humans to live once on this earth and after that comes the judgment. Nobody is allowed to come back after death in another form as trees, birds, animals or humans for a second chance.

It is while we are alive that we have the choice to accept salvation, "that Jesus died on the Cross for you." He was the perfect Sacrifice for you and me so we could have eternal life.

A new body will be given to us at the resurrection with our same spirit and soul. With Jesus, we will be blessed and happy forever because we will be in His presence for eternity in Paradise.

When I Die

Have you ever asked yourself the question, "When I die, where am I going for eternity? Can we know now?"

Our life on the earth is temporary, it has been lent to us, and one day we will all have to be judged in front of our Creator God.

Jesus came to give His life for ours; He made a Way for us. This is the only way to have the assurance in our heart that we will be saved and have our place with Jesus for eternity.

When we accepted Jesus in our heart and in our lives, we received the Holy Spirit of God and we became born again Christians, children of God.

As we read His Words in the Bible, we renew our mind in the truth and our strength grows day by day. We reject everything that Satan, the enemy, tries to deceive us with—his lies.

You are more than a conqueror when you decide to invite Jesus in your heart as your personal Saviour and Lord. Jesus gives us the assurance of Eternity with Him.

It is a free gift from God our Father in Heaven. Nothing will ever separate us from the Love of God.

"For God so loved the world that He gave His only begotten Son, that whoever believes in Him should not perish but have everlasting life." John 3:16

Thank You

In the morning, when I wake up, I say to you thank you. Thank you for my life and thank you for my rest.

I start my day with You because without You, I would not be. You gave me life and love so I can live day by day.

My spirit and my thoughts are focused on You because Jesus, You are my everything. Make my life filled with Your Spirit so I can do the work that You have prepared for me.

Make my words always speak your truth for everyone who will hear me. I want to be for You a messenger for everyone that You send me.

May that I never be ashamed to testify of my faith for you and that I can tell the whole world that Jesus is King.

When You died on the cross for our sins, You have accomplished everything and we have to believe it by faith.

My Love

My love, my friend, I want to be with you. Wherever I am, you are near me.

In the morning, when I wake up, I would not be the same, if you would not be there to wrap me in your arms.

So many years went by, and we are still there for each other. The Lord has blessed us and we know that He is the One who helps us every day.

We know that one day we will be separated when the Lord comes to take one of us. But it will be just for a time because we will be together again when we both go back into the Presence of the Lord, in His home that He prepares for us for eternity.

There is no place on this earth that I would want to be without you.

Every day when we have battles or struggles, we let Jesus help us with His strength and we grow every day in His Love.

Message of God

The other day, I went for a ride in the country and that is when the Lord gave me a message to share with my entire neighbourhood.

He told me: "Tell them that I am God in Heaven and without Me, there is no other God. All other gods are false. I am the God of eternity who reigns in heaven. I have loved you all and I gave you My Son, Jesus Christ, who is God to save you. Call upon His Name to forgive you and He will give you eternal life. It is I who created heaven and earth, all the universe and the seas. I gave all humans the breath of life so that they would be Mine, whom I have chosen. It is I who paid the price, and the only thing you have to say is "Yes" to be with Me in paradise, and be happy forever and ever."

Why Don't You Take the Time?

Take the time

Take the time

It is so important

To take the time.

Stop and think

Of your Eternity

Ask yourself

What must I do to be saved?

You only have to ask Him

It is a free gift.

You only have to accept Him

In your heart to be saved.

When you believe by faith

That He died on the Cross.

A perfect sacrifice done for you.

Jesus Christ you are the King.

Don't live playing games.

The decision has to be made by you.

It is not when you will be dead

Because it will be too late.

Take the time to worship Him.

Take the time to pray to Him.

Take the time to thank Him.

Take the time to adore Him.

After life comes the Judgment

If you accepted Him with all your heart

He saved you with assurance

And you will get your crown.

"Let the word of Christ dwell in you richly in all wisdom, teaching and admonishing one another in palms and hymns and spiritual songs, singing with grace in your hearts to the Lord."
Colossians 3:16

Put Your Trust in Me

I put my trust in you God, my Creator, because my life without you has no value. I could ask for all the wealth of the world but it is in my heart that I found true happiness.

Why is there so many people that I would like to talk about You, my Saviour, my only Truth? There are only a few people who take the time to stop and think about their eternity.

My heart is troubled when it comes the time to celebrate for there is nobody to share Your Word of Truth. They talk of everything and it's for nothing. Why don't they take the time now while they still have time?

All those words are for us to think that life is only temporary, it is lent to us. We don't have time to waste; we have to think because that day will come. Let us know the day when we will be asked to see our Creator, God our Saviour.

The Freedom

You, my friend, who have anxiety, you don't have the strength to free yourself. Every day of your life, you fear and have a hard time to have true happiness in your heart.

You put your mind on your problems and it is what is destroying you. Fear doesn't come from God. Trust in Him and you will be set free and healed.

When the worries of life come in your mind, you have the power to reject it. Call upon Jesus' Name in your heart, and you will have the strength to keep your mind positive.

The Word of God is your sword to destroy the enemy. If you put God's Word deep down in your heart and your spirit, you will have the victory over fear and your faith will grow.

Every time you call upon Jesus' Name, He is there to help you.

Song
The Little Nic Nic

It is the Little Nic Nic

Who was singing at the restaurant?

To all her good clients

It was always a joy

For her to share her faith.

For her to share her faith.

When she was singing in her heart

She gave thanks to the Lord.

And when she was looking at a flower,

She noticed His greatness.

When she was praying

And she was asking

Why, to the Living God

His love is so deep.

When she was talking of Jesus

Everywhere she was going

To everyone who believes

The Holy Spirit they receive.

It is His blood on the Cross

That Jesus gave for you and me

And when we walk by faith

We find real joy.

The Little Nic Nic gives us that song

That we may stop and think

That Jesus saves us

And we should give Him thanks.

Come To Me

You My child who have pain
Why don't you listen to My voice?
I want so much that you come back
So that I can give you My joy.

The worries and the struggles of this life
Make you forsake Me.
It is in those days that I am close to you
Just listen to Me and hear My voice.

I am for you a True Friend
Wherever you are, I hear your call
I am the only One who can console you
Because My Word is Truth.

If you walk near Me,
I will set you free.
You will have My Holy Spirit
And you will have within you True life.

There is no other
That knows you better than Me.
The day that you will come back to Me,
I will heal you from all your pain.

Take courage, don't worry.
Come to Me, I am waiting for you.
I want to wrap you in My arms.
I open My arms to you. Feel my Love.

"For God so loved the world that He gave His only begotten Son, that whoever believes in Him should not perish but have everlasting Life."

John 3:16

Anxiety

There are so many things that oppress me throughout my life. I need someone to tell me what to do to set me free.

These problems come to haunt my soul and I don't know what to do. This anxiety creates in my life a lot of health problems. I have a hard time to sleep and to digest my food.

I need a solution to my problems. Who can give it to me? I can't achieve it by myself.

One day, I shared this with my friend and she replied to me: "Give it to Jesus Christ, put your trust in Him. He will give you True Life."

In His love, He will strengthen you every day if you give Him all your cares. But if you doubt in your heart, there is nothing He can do for you because you let the enemy take control of your mind.

It is Jesus who paid the price when He died for you. He told us in His Word of Truth: "I will be with you. Trust in Me and you will have real joy. Read and meditate on My Word for the truth will be in you in abundance."

You have to trust in Him and in all circumstances. Whenever the enemy tries to worry you, there is nothing that is too big for God to handle."

After I talked with my friend, I realized that Jesus was the **only** answer. Without Him in my life, I could not be free of the anxiety that wants to attack and take control of my life.

The enemy Satan has a stronghold on me. He makes me doubt so I don't put my trust in Jesus. But I am the only one who has to win the struggle by putting all my faith in You, Lord Jesus Christ, my King and my Saviour.

"…casting all your care upon Him, for He cares for you." 1 Peter 5:7

How to Define Bullying: Physically and Mentally

Many times, the bullying is a form of insult; it can be physical or stealing of lunches at school from other people around us. Sometimes it is all year long, day after day by one person or a group of people.

This brings shame, depression and even suicide from the one who is being bullied. They don't want to share it with anybody because they isolate themselves and are scared.

How do we react against our bullies? As long that they see that you are afraid, they will continue bullying you. We should not seek revenge but to show them love, which is the best way to respond. Keep your joy and look at them with a smile and don't say a word. Your behaviour will bring something positive.

Through God's eyes, you are precious. When you know who you are in Jesus and you take the Word of God in your heart, you have the armour of God in you.

1. **Explanation about your worth in God's eyes:**

    That means that you know who you are. God loves you with an unconditional love. He gave you Jesus to save you and forgive all your sins. He wants you to put all your trust in Him, to give Him your life and He wants your heart to worship Him. He will take all your fears and He will give you freedom if you trust Him.

2. **Who are you in Jesus?**

    If you give your life to Jesus and accept Him as your personal Saviour and Lord of your life, He will live in you and His Holy Spirit will dwell in you. You are a child of God.

3. **Word of truth:**

    The Bible is the Word of God that gives you strength and the power to forgive. Do not let anybody tell you otherwise. You are loved by God and nobody can take that from you.

4. Put on your armour of God:

When you read the Bible, the Truth comes to live within you. The Word of God gives you His armour to defend you against negative things coming into your life. You don't need to let other people destroy your life with things or words that do not belong to you. The negative words come from Satan who is trying to destroy you. If somebody tries to assault or abuse you physically, tell someone about it. Don't keep it to yourself. Tell a teacher, parents or friends. The authority is there for you! Take it!

Do not blame yourself and keep everything on your shoulders, thinking it is you who has a problem. This is only a lie from the enemy. It does not belong to you. The enemy is there to destroy you.

The bully is trying to control you and doesn't know that he is miserable and needs help himself. Bullies need the Love of God in their lives, and need Jesus. Everybody will have to face the Judgment in the end for all they did, good or bad, in their lives.

Those who don't repent of their sins will be without God for eternity. But the ones who keep their heart pure before God will have eternal life with God, Jesus Christ and the Holy Spirit.

"Put on the whole armour of God, that you may be able to stand against the wiles of devil."
Ephesians 6:11

Prayer to be Saved

Lord Jesus, I need You in my life.

Today, I accept You as my Saviour.

I acknowledge you, Jesus as God, and my Lord and Saviour

And I know that I am a sinner

And I ask You for forgiveness for all my sins.

Thank You for forgiving me

Thank You for changing me.

Transform me by Your Holy Spirit

And by the Truth of Your Word.

I want to live for You every day of my life

And to be a witness of Your love.

Today, I am born again, born of Your Spirit.

Thank you, Jesus, for saving me.

And every day of my life

I want to thank You, worship You and adore You.

The End of my Book

Every word of this book has been inspired while I was fishing at the Blanche River during the months of May 2013 and May 2014.

With my pen and a piece of paper, I wrote everything that came in to my spirit.

Today, I want to share it with you with all my love and I hope it will bless you. Amen.